Collins

English

KS1 Revision
English

Age
5 – 7

Key Stage 1

Revision
Guide

Wendy Arnold

Contents

Contents

Letters, Sounds and Words

- Recognise different sounds for letters
- Understand how letters and sounds make words
- Understand how the letter 'e' at the end of a word affects the vowel sound.

Letters and Sounds

The **letters** in the alphabet represent sounds. Each letter has a name and a sound.

Example

A a apple    **S s** strawberry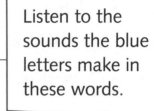

> Listen to the sounds the blue letters make in these words.

Sometimes, two or three letters are put together to make one sound.

Example

- 'sh' is one sound but two letters work together to make the sound.
- 'ch' is one sound but two letters work together to make the sound.
- 'ea' is one sound but two letters work together to make the sound.

> **Key Point**
>
> Some words have two or more letters which make one sound.

Sounds and Words

Sounds are used together to make **words**.

Example

- if ← Two letters, two sounds
- sit ← Three letters, three sounds
- shut ← Four letters but three sounds
- eat ← Three letters but two sounds

Words with Different Sounds

Sometimes, the same letter can make different sounds in different words.

Example

g = The **g**entle **g**iant has some **g**old.

c = The **c**at lives in the shopping **c**entre in the **c**ity.

The same letter can make different sounds in different words.

Letter 'e' at the End of Words

When the letter **'e'** is at the end of a word, it often changes the first **vowel sound** in the word from a short vowel sound to a long vowel sound. It makes the **vowel** say its name.

Example

Look at how the 'e' at the end of these words changes the first vowel sound:

- hop → hope
- pin → pine
- tap → tape
- bit → bite

Tip

You can think of the 'e' at the end of these words as **magic 'e'**, because it changes the sound of the vowel, e.g. bit → bite.

Quick Test

1. The word 'chip' has four letters. How many sounds does it have?
2. Listen to the sound that the letter 'g' makes in these words. Circle the odd one out.

   game   **get**   **gem**   **girl**
3. Add the magic 'e' to these words:

   a) fat

   b) kit

Key Words

- Letter
- Word
- Vowel sound
- Vowel

Sounds and Syllables

- Read words with one syllable and more than one syllable
- Understand how to break words into syllables

Reading Words with One Syllable

Syllables are like 'beats' in words. Every syllable has a **vowel sound**.

Example

The vowel sounds in these words are shown in blue:

it dad got can kid get bug sell

> Each of these words has one syllable.

Read these sentences and clap the syllables.

'Let me tell you a tale of Pat the dog', said Miss Blow to the class.

'One day, Pat the dog got up. 'Let's go!' said Pat.

And off he went'.

Short words usually have one syllable; longer words tend to have more.

Key Point

Most words contain at least one **vowel** (a, e, i, o, u). In some words the vowel sound is made by 'y'.

Reading Words with Two Syllables

Some words have two syllables or 'beats'. Each syllable has a vowel sound.

Tip

Clapping helps you to hear where the syllables or 'beats' are.

Example

journey chickens spiders started

Look at where the syllables are:

jour/ney chick/ens spi/ders start/ed

> Each of these words has two syllables.

Read these sentences and clap the syllables.

> On his jour/ney Pat the dog saw chi/ckens on a farm and lots of spi/ders in the barn.
>
> It start/ed to rain. The chi/ckens flew up to the barn roof.

Words with More Syllables

Some words have three or more syllables.

Example

yes/ter/day

com/pu/ter ← Each of these words has three syllables.

Sep/tem/ber

Read these sentences and clap the syllables.

> Pat the dog con/tin/ued on his ad/ven/ture.
>
> Sudd/en/ly he re/al/ised it was Sat/ur/day.
>
> 'Time to go home', said Pat the dog.

Tip

To learn a word, break the word into syllables to remember it, e.g. ba-by, Sep-tem-ber.

Quick Test

1. What is a syllable?
2. Say a word that has:
   a) one syllable
   b) two syllables
   c) three syllables
3. How many syllables are there in the word 'holiday'?

Key Words

- Syllable
- Vowel sound
- Vowel

Apostrophes

- Understand that the apostrophe can replace letters when words are joined together
- Understand that the apostrophe can show belonging

Apostrophes to show Missing Letters

Sometimes, two words can be joined together. When this happens, letters are taken out and are replaced by an **apostrophe**.

Example

She has ➤ She's — The apostrophe replaces the letters 'ha'.

He will ➤ He'll — The apostrophe replaces the letters 'wi'.

Key Point

An apostrophe takes the place of the missing letters.

Read this part of the fairy tale *Sleeping Beauty* and look for shortened words with an apostrophe.

Once upon a time a good King and Queen had a baby daughter. All the fairies of the land were invited to a party, but one old fairy wasn't invited. She was very angry. She came to the party and said, 'When the Princess is sixteen she'll touch a spindle and die!'

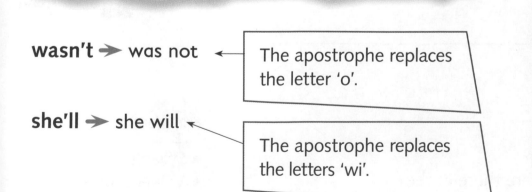

wasn't ➤ was not — The apostrophe replaces the letter 'o'.

she'll ➤ she will — The apostrophe replaces the letters 'wi'.

Tip

will not → won't
shall not → shan't
These don't fit the rule for apostrophes. This is because it would be hard to say 'willn't' or shalln't'!

Apostrophes to Show Belonging

An apostrophe can be used to show who, or what, something belongs to.

Example

The queen's baby ← The baby belongs to the queen.

The king's land ← The land belongs to the king.

Read this story and look for apostrophes of belonging.

The good fairies made lovely wishes. But the bad fairy's wish was for the Princess to die. The good fairies could not stop the wish but they could change it. They changed the wish to everyone sleeping for a hundred years.

Then a Prince arrived and everyone woke up. The Prince and Princess got married and rode away to the Prince's kingdom far, far away.

'**fairy's wish**' = the wish belongs to the fairy

'**Prince's kingdom**' = the kingdom belongs to the Prince

Key Point

Apostrophe + s ('s) shows that an item belongs to a place, person or thing.

Quick Test

1. What letter is replaced by the apostrophe in the word 'He's'?
2. Join these words together using an apostrophe:
   a) I will
   b) is not
   c) it is
3. Put the apostrophe in this sentence:
   The fairys wish was good.

Key Word

- Apostrophe

Suffixes

- Read words ending in *–ing* and *–ed*
- Read words ending in *–s*, *–es*, *–er* and *–est*

Suffixes

A **suffix** is a **letter** or group of letters added to the end of a word to make a new word.

Reading Words Ending in *–ing*

When a word ends in 'e', you take off the 'e' before adding 'ing'.

> **Tip**
>
> When a word ends in 'e', you must take off the 'e' before you add 'ing', 'ed', 'es', 'er' or 'est'.

Example

squeeze + **ing** = squeezing

Read this description of a character from *A Christmas Carol* by Charles Dickens.

Scrooge! A squeez**ing**, wrench**ing**, grasp**ing**, scrap**ing**, clutch**ing** old man!

> Squeeze and scrape have both had the 'e' taken off before adding 'ing'.

Reading Words Ending in *–ed*

Many words can have the suffix *–ed* added to them, to make new words.

The *–ed* ending makes different sounds in different words. It can sound like *'t'*, *'d'* or *'id'*.

Example

Read this text.

The cold froze his old features, nipp**ed** his point**ed** nose, shrivell**ed** his cheek, stiffen**ed** his walk …

Words ending in *–ed* with the '*t*' sound	Words ending in *–ed* with the '*d*' sound	Words ending in *–ed* with the '*id*' sound
nipp**ed**	shrivell**ed** stiffen**ed**	point**ed**

Reading Words Ending in *–s* and *–es*

The suffix *–s* can sound like '*s*' or '*z*'. The suffix *–es* can sound like '*es*' or '*ez*'. Using the suffix *–es* adds an extra **syllable** or 'beat' to a word.

Example

Scrooge had box**es** of money, but no friend**s**.

> Adding *–es* to this word gives it an extra syllable.

> Adding *–s* to this word gives it a 'z' sound.

Reading Words Ending in *–er* and *–est*

Some words can have the suffixes *–er* or *–est* added to them. When a word ends in 'e', you take off the 'e' before adding 'er' or 'est'.

Example

Bob Cratchit worked for Scrooge. He was poor**er** than Scrooge.

Scrooge was the mean**est** person anyone knew.

After a dream, Scrooge became the kind**est** person anyone knew!

Quick Test

1. Add *–ing* to the word 'care'.
2. Add *–er* and *–est* to the word 'nice'.
3. Add *–es* or *–s* to these words:
   a) fox **b)** bridge

Key Words

- Suffix
- Letter
- Syllable

Common Exception Words

- Read common exception words
- Read plural exception words

Reading Common Exception Words

Common **exception words** are tricky words where one or more letter does not make its usual sound.

Exception words are usually words you see and hear quite a lot.

Example

- Most short words ending in the 's' sound are spelt 'ss' (e.g. me**ss**, cla**ss**, fu**ss**), but 'bus' ends in just one 's' so it is an exception word.
- The word 'school' has a 'ch' in it, but makes a sound like 'k'. So it is an exception word.
- The word 'sugar' is an exception word because it starts with an 's', but the 's' is pronounced 'sh'.

The best way to learn the exception words (or tricky words) is to read and write them lots of times.

Look at the word	Say it	Cover it up	Write it	Check it
school	school	school	school	✓

Remembering Exception Words

It might help you to group words that are similar. Can you see any patterns or words that have the same sounds?

Key Point

Exception words tend to contain one or more letters that does not make its usual sound.

Example

<u>o</u>ld, c<u>o</u>ld, g<u>o</u>ld, h<u>o</u>ld, t<u>o</u>ld ← The letter 'o' has the long vowel sound in all these words even though the words don't end in 'e'.

find, mind, behind ← The letter 'i' has the long vowel sound in all these words even though the words don't end in 'e'.

Revise

These are all exception words. They don't follow the usual spelling pattern, but they can be put in groups that have the same sound.

Tip

Some of the exception words can be grouped. Try to put similar words in groups and keep a list so you remember.

Plural Exception Words

To change most words from **singular** (one) to **plural** (more than one) the rule is normally to add an 's' to the word.

Example

- one cat ➤ two cat**s**
- one dog ➤ four dog**s**

But some plural words do not end in 's'. These are exception words:

Example

- one **foot** ➤ two **feet**
- one **man** ➤ two **men**
- There was one **child** running down the corridor. The rest of the **children** were walking.
- There was one cheeky **mouse** nibbling at the cheese, while the other **mice** watched.

Quick Test

1. What does plural mean?
2. What does singular mean?
3. What is the plural of 'person'?

Key Words

- Exception words
- Singular
- Plural

Compound Words

- Identify compound words

Compound Words

Compound words are two words used together to make another word.

Example

sun + set = **sunset** → Two words make this word.

afternoon ← afternoon = after + noon

teapot ← teapot = tea + pot

football ← football = foot + ball

hairbrush ← hairbrush = hair + brush

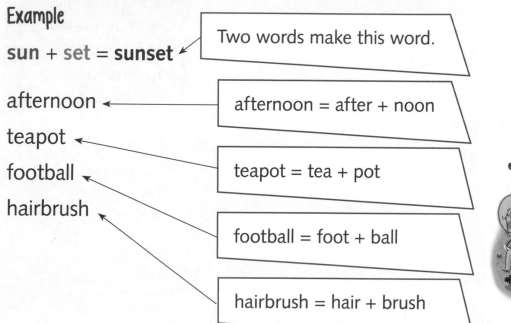

Most compound words are pronounced the way you would expect, but some sound different.

Example

Read the words and then the compound words and listen to the difference:
- band + age = bandage
- cup + board = cupboard

Quick Test

1. Which words have been joined to make compound words?
   a) bedroom   **b)** airport   **c)** hillside
2. Add a word to each of these to make a compound word:
   a) sea   **b)** fire   **c)** play

Key Word

- Compound word

Practice Questions

Challenge 1

G) Grammar   P) Punctuation   S) Spelling

GS **1** Read the sentences. Change the words in bold into one word by removing one letter and adding an apostrophe. Write the shortened word.

a) **I am** so happy.

_____

b) **We are** happy too.

_____

2 marks

P **2** Read the sentences and add the apostrophe to the word in bold to show belonging.

a) The Princess was the **Queens** baby.

b) It was the bad **fairys** spindle.

2 marks

Challenge 2

G **1** Read the sentences and circle the correct word.

a) Scrooge **looked / looking** mean.

b) Bob Cratchit **cared / caring** for his son, Tiny Tim.

c) Scrooge was **change / changing**.

3 marks

Challenge 3

1 Read the words. Clap the syllables. Draw lines to separate the syllables.

a) D e c e m b e r

b) r o o f t o p

2 marks

2 Add a word to each of these to make compound words.

a) sun _____

b) snow _____

c) key _____

3 marks

Poetry

- Read classic and contemporary poems
- Recognise riddles and rhymes
- Recognise tongue twisters

Classic Poems

A **poem** can describe a feeling or object, tell a story or joke, or just play with words.

Rhyme is when words have the same end sound. Rhyming words are often at the end of the lines.

Rhythm is the 'beat' in the lines of a poem.

Classic poems often have a regular rhyme and rhythm.

> **Key Point**
>
> Rhyming words have endings that sound the same. They usually appear at the end of each line of a poem.

Example

The Owl and the Pussy-cat went to sea
In a beautiful pea green boat.
They took some honey, and plenty of money,
Wrapped up in a five pound note.

The word 'boat' rhymes with 'note' in the last line.

The words 'honey' and 'money' rhyme.

Contemporary Poems

Contemporary poems are modern poems. They are usually written in **free verse**. This means that they do not have a regular rhyme or rhythm.

Example

The tree was sad,
Leaves falling,
Bare branches,
Against the moon.

16

Riddles and Rhymes

A **riddle** is a kind of puzzle. It gives clues. You have to work out what it means.

Example

I have a face and two hands, but no legs. What am I? A clock!

A rhyme has words with the same sounds at the end of the lines.

Example

Monday's child is fair of **face**,

Tuesday's child is full of **grace**,

Tongue Twisters

Tongue twisters are fun phrases or sentences that use **alliteration**. Alliteration is when you repeat the same first letter or sound in a sequence of words. It is what makes tongue twisters tricky to say!

Example

- **She** **s**ells **s**ea**sh**ells on the **s**ea**sh**ore.
- **B**etty **B**otter **b**ought some **b**utter. '**B**ut', she said, 'the **b**utter's **b**itter'.

Repeats the sounds 's' and 'sh'.

Repeats the letter 'b'.

Key Words

- Poem
- Rhyme
- Rhythm
- Free verse
- Riddle
- Tongue twister
- Alliteration

Quick Test

1. Where are rhyming words usually found in a poem?
2. What is a riddle?
3. Which of these words rhyme with 'sea'?
   me   top   tree   car   saw   key

Fiction: Stories

- Understand key stories
- Understand fairy stories
- Understand traditional tales

Understanding Key Stories

A **key story** is a **fiction** story (a made-up story) that has been written recently. It may be an adventure, a mystery or a science fiction story.

All good stories start with a problem. There is a cause, an effect and at the end, a solution. An easy way to remember this is:

WHAT (problem) → WHY (cause) → WHERE/WHO (effect) → HOW (solution)

A story could be about people, animals, aliens, trolls, invented creatures, ghosts or other things.

Some stories are funny, others are sad. They can tell you about a made-up creature, a friendship or an adventure.

Storybooks often have wonderful pictures to help you understand the meaning of the story.

Key Point

Good stories always have a problem, a cause, an effect and a solution.

Understanding Fairy Stories

A **fairy story** is a type of short story that usually has dwarves, elves, fairies, giants, gnomes, goblins, mermaids, trolls or witches in it, and usually magic or spells.

Example

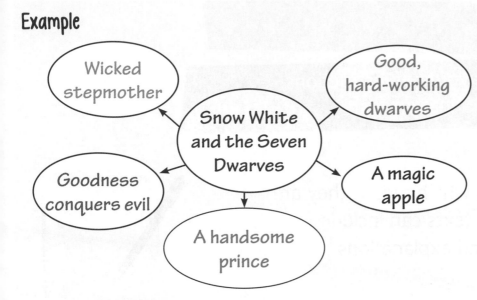

Wicked stepmother

Good, hard-working dwarves

Snow White and the Seven Dwarves

Goodness conquers evil

A magic apple

A handsome prince

Understanding Traditional Tales

A **traditional tale** is an old story. Traditional tales often teach a lesson or give a moral message and pass on ideas.

Example

- *Goldilocks and the Three Bears* – don't use things that don't belong to you.

- *The Tortoise and the Hare* – slow and steady wins the race.

- *Three Billy Goats Gruff* – don't be greedy (like the troll); face your fears (crossing the bridge).

The characters in a traditional tale can be human or animals. Some characters are good and some are bad. The youngest character is often a hero. Often there are three events, wishes or challenges.

Tip

When you are reading a story, look for the good and bad characters. Is there any magic? Can you find the problem?

Quick Test

1. What features do all good stories have?
2. What kind of characters are there in a fairy story?
3. What message is given in *Goldilocks and the Three Bears*?

Key Words

- Key story
- Fiction
- Fairy story
- Traditional tale

Non-fiction

- Recognise features and layouts of instructions, information texts and explanation texts

Non-fiction

Some texts are **non-fiction**, which means they are based on facts. Non-fiction texts can include **instructions**, **information** and explanations.

Instructions

Some texts give instructions on how to do something. They often have the following features:

- a list of equipment needed
- numbered, simple, clear instructions or rules
- diagrams or pictures to help understanding
- **commands**, e.g. cut the paper, chop the onion
- a goal.

Example

Four castle corners

This is a game for the whole class.
You need a classroom and a chair. ← Equipment needed
Label each of the classroom corners: dungeon, ← tower, courtyard and hall. ← Commands ('Label...' 'Choose...')

1. Choose one person to sit in the middle of ← the class on the royal throne.

2. The person on the throne closes their eyes ← and counts to ten. → Instructions

3. Everyone else chooses a corner.

4. The person on the throne calls out a corner – those people in that corner are out.

5. Keep going until there is a winner. ← Command ('keep...')

The goal is to be crowned king or queen and ← sit on the royal throne. → The goal of the game.

Information

Some texts give information. A text giving information might have the following features:

- short bullet points and lists
- pictures or diagrams
- **headings** with small chunks of writing
- an **index, glossary** or **contents** page.

Example

Penguins

- There are 17 different kinds of penguin.
- An adult Emperor penguin travels 200 kilometres in the late autumn.

Emperor penguin

Key Point

Instructions tell you how to do something. Information texts give you details.

This information text has a heading, bullet points and a picture.

Explanations

Some texts tell you how and why something happens. An explanation text might have the following features:

- numbered points
- pictures or diagrams
- instructions on how to do things.

Key Point

Explanations tell you how and why something happens.

Example

How Bees Make Honey

1.
Bees drink nectar from flowers.

2.
Bees have long tongues. They suck up the nectar.

3.
Bees spit the nectar into cells in the hive.

This explanation has pictures and numbered points.

Key Words

- Non-fiction
- Instructions
- Information
- Commands
- Headings
- Index
- Glossary
- Contents

Quick Test

1. What kind of words are used in instructions?
2. What kind of text is most likely to have a glossary?
3. What kind of texts tell you how and why?

Literary Language

- Recognise recurring language in fairy stories and traditional tales
- Recognise recurring language in poetry

Recurring Language in Fairy and Traditional Stories

Fairy stories and **traditional tales** share some **recurring** (or repeated) language and themes. They often start and end with certain words or phrases.

Example

'Once upon a time …'

'They lived happily ever after …'.

Fairy stories and traditional tales usually have good and evil characters.

Fairy stories also often have:
- Royalty, such as a castle, a prince, a princess, a king and a queen.
- Poverty, such as a poor family or a poor shepherd.
- Magic and spells.
- Imaginary characters, such as fairies, trolls, elves and goblins.

Fairy stories tend to repeat words and sentences.

Example

Language is repeated in *Cinderella*:

> She tried on the slipper, but it was too big.
>
> She tried on the slipper, but it was too small.
>
> She tried on the slipper and it was just right.

Words and sentences are repeated in *Cinderella*.

Traditional tales also repeat language in order to help the reader to get involved and repeat the words with the storyteller.

Example

The question words 'Who's been . . .?' are repeated throughout the story *Goldilocks and The Three Bears*. For example:
- 'Who's been eating my porridge?'
- 'Who's been sitting in my chair?'

Recurring Language in Poetry

Recurring language can be used in poetry to make something stand out.

Adjectives are describing words which make you think of feelings, or how things look.

Example

In the **dark, dark** woods there's a **dark, dark** cave.

The adjective 'dark' describes how a wood or cave looks, but it could also mean spooky or scary.

Key Point

Recurring language in stories or poems makes you want to join in and gives you a picture inside your head.

Key Point

Adjectives are used a lot in poetry to describe feelings or how something looks.

Key Words

- Fairy story
- Traditional tale
- Recurring language
- Adjective

Quick Test

1. Give a phrase that appears in traditional tales and fairy stories.
2. What are describing words called?

Finding and Commenting on Words

- Understand alphabetical order
- Use a dictionary
- Scan for information

Alphabetical Order

Alphabetical order is when you put words in an order depending on the first letter in the word.

a b c d e f g h i j k l m n o p q r s t u v w x y z

Example

These names of rivers are not in alphabetical order:
Nile, Thames, Ganges, Mississippi, Amazon, Andes

Now they are in alphabetical order:
Amazon, Andes, Ganges, Mississippi, Nile, Thames

Alphabetical order is used for indexes in books, for the names on a class register and in **dictionaries**.

Learning alphabetical order will help you to use a dictionary.

Key Point

It is important to know the alphabet to help you put words in alphabetical order.

Using a Dictionary

It is useful to use a dictionary to help you to understand the meaning of words. Dictionaries list words and explain what they mean. The words are listed in alphabetical order to help you to find them.

Example

Using a dictionary can help you find the meaning of words like 'rust' in the sentence below.

The Eiffel Tower in Paris, France, is painted every seven years to protect it from <u>rust</u>.

A dictionary will tell you that rust = metal that has been destroyed by water or air.

24

Your answers to these questions should be similar to these:

1. He is called 'Little John' as a friendly joke because he is so big.
2. He would not let Robin Hood cross the bridge because he wanted to play with him.
   We think this because he is a playful character and he lets Robin Hood cross the bridge after a while.

Ask yourself questions as you read a text to help you to understand what you are reading.

Predicting What Will Happen

When you have read part of a text, you can sometimes **predict** (work out what is going to happen next), based on the information in the text and your own knowledge.

Key Point

Predicting is working out what might happen next.

Example

Maid Marion and Robin Hood fell in love. One day they met a monk. His name was Friar Tuck. He said he would only marry Robin Hood and Maid Marion if Robin Hood could answer a riddle.

What do you think happens next?

You could predict from this text that Robin Hood answers the riddle and marries Maid Marion.

Quick Test

1. What does 'predict' mean?
2. Fill in the gaps in this sentence:
   You need to read the _____, look at the _____ and think carefully before coming to a conclusion.

Key Word

• Predict

Practice Questions

Challenge 1

1 Read the words and put them in alphabetical order.

octopus   antelope   whale   caterpillar   tiger

_____

_____

5 marks

Challenge 2

1 Tick the language and themes found in fairy stories and traditional tales.

a) Once upon a time … ☐

b) A spider is an arachnid. ☐

c) The lifecycle of a butterfly ☐

d) a castle, a prince, a king ☐

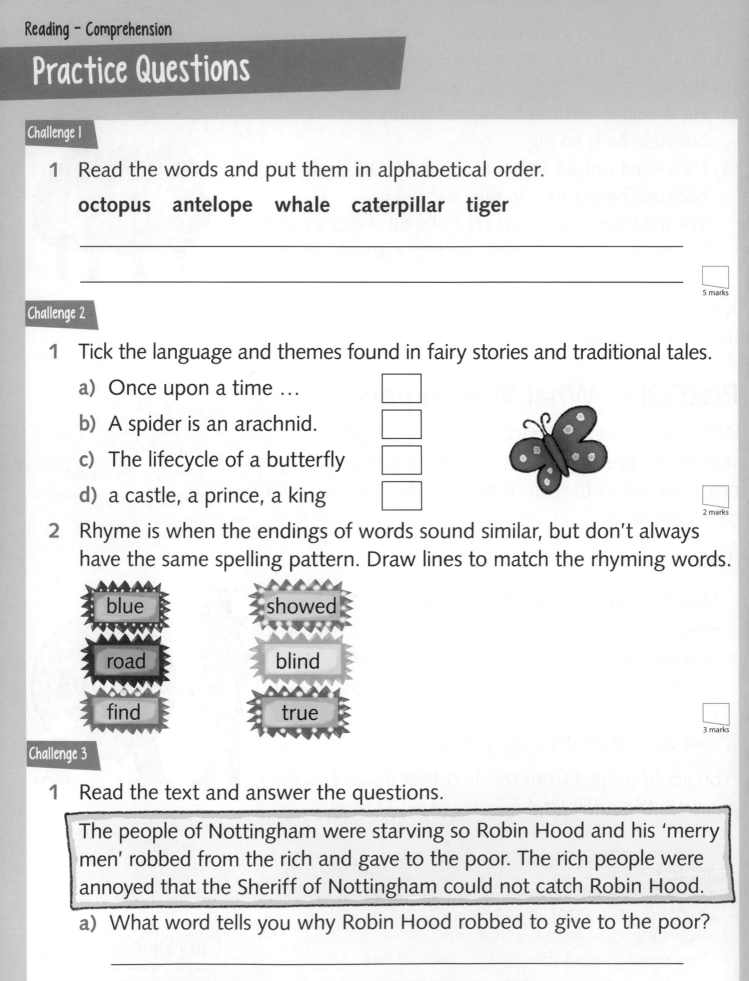

2 marks

2 Rhyme is when the endings of words sound similar, but don't always have the same spelling pattern. Draw lines to match the rhyming words.

blue   showed

road   blind

find   true

3 marks

Challenge 3

1 Read the text and answer the questions.

> The people of Nottingham were starving so Robin Hood and his 'merry men' robbed from the rich and gave to the poor. The rich people were annoyed that the Sheriff of Nottingham could not catch Robin Hood.

a) What word tells you why Robin Hood robbed to give to the poor?

_____

b) What word tells you how the rich people felt?

_____

2 marks

Review Questions

| G | Grammar | P | Punctuation | S | Spelling |

G **1** Write the two words that make up these compound words.

    a) butterfly   _____ + _____

    b) blackberry   _____ + _____

    c) playground   _____ + _____

    d) whiteboard   _____ + _____

    e) football   _____ + _____   5 marks

2 Draw lines to match the words that begin with the same sounds.

phone	**j**am
gentle	**f**inger
city	**sh**oe
sugar	**k**itchen
chemist	**s**nake

5 marks

G **3** Read the pairs of words. Underline the plurals.

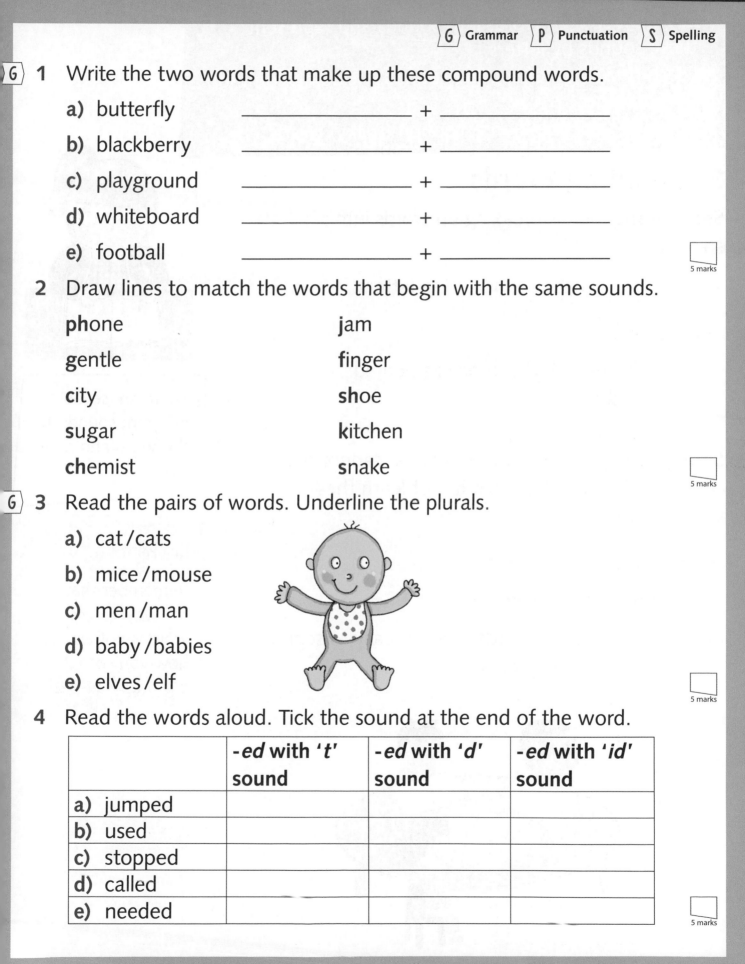

    a) cat / cats

    b) mice / mouse

    c) men / man

    d) baby / babies

    e) elves / elf   5 marks

4 Read the words aloud. Tick the sound at the end of the word.

	-*ed* with '*t*' sound	-*ed* with '*d*' sound	-*ed* with '*id*' sound
a) jumped			
b) used			
c) stopped			
d) called			
e) needed			

5 marks

Spelling Sounds and Homophones

- Segment spoken words into sounds and represent these sounds by letters
- Learn new ways of spelling sounds, including common homophones
- Learn to spell common exception (tricky) words

Segmenting Words

Segmenting means breaking up words into separate sounds.

You can write these sounds using **letters**.

Example

The word 'yesterday' can be segmented:

y-e-s-t-er-d-ay

Some exception words (tricky words) cannot be segmented easily. You have to just learn these as whole words.

Example

was   the   tired   saw   to

There are exception words. It is not easy to segment the sounds in these words.

There are seven different sounds in this word and nine letters.

Key Point

Remember that the way you say a word is not always how you spell it, e.g. was = w-o-z

Spelling Sounds

The spellings of sounds can be different.

Example

'Photo' and 'film' both have an 'f' sound but different letters are used to make the sound.

'Kite' and 'cat' both have a 'k' sound but different letters are used to make the sound.

Homophones

Two words might sound exactly the same, but different letters are used to spell them and the words have different meanings. These words are called **homophones**.

Example

there / their

here / hear

bare / bear ← These pairs of words sound the same but are spelt differently and mean different things.

blue / blew

night / knight

sea / see

> ### Tip
>
> Think about what the words mean in a sentence, e.g. 'I can hear you!' makes sense, but 'I can here you!' does not make sense.

Quick Test

1. What does segmenting mean?
2. What are homophones?
3. How many sounds are in the word 'cup'?
4. How many sounds are in the word 'shop'?

Key Words

- Segmenting
- Letter
- Homophone

Using Suffixes and Prefixes

- Use suffixes *–ing*, *-ed*, *-ment*, *-ness*
- Add *–s* or *–es* for nouns and third person
- Use the prefix *–un*

Suffixes *–ing* and *–ed*

A **suffix** is added to the end of a word to make a new word. Some common suffixes are *–ing* and *-ed*. These suffixes can be added to **verbs** ('doing' words) to change their meaning

Example

Adding *–ing* to a verb allows you to write about something that is happening or was happening in the present or past.

- pull ⟶ pull**ing**   (e.g. He is pulling the door).
- hope ⟶ hop**ing** (e.g. She was hoping it would work).

> For words ending in 'e' drop the 'e' before adding *-ing*.

Adding *–ed* to a verb allows you to write about what happened in the past.

- shock ⟶ shock**ed**
- pull ⟶ pull**ed**

If a word contains a short vowel sound, you often need to double the last letter of the word before adding *–ing* or *–ed*:

- di**g** ⟶ di**gg**ing
- cla**p** ⟶ cla**pp**ed

Tip

Never double the 'x' before adding a suffix, e.g. mixing, mixed.

Suffixes *–ment* and *–ness*

The suffixes *–ment* and *–ness* can be added to a verb or an **adjective** to change its meaning. This turns the verb or adjective into a **noun**.

Key Point

A suffix is added to the end of a word to make a new word.

Example

- excite ⟶ excite**ment** ⟵ Verb turns into a noun

• cheerful ⟶ cheerful**ness** ← Adjective turns into a noun

Suffixes –s and –es

The suffixes –s and –es are often added to the end of words to make them **plural**.

Example

promise ⟶ promise**s**

torch ⟶ torch**es** ← Words ending with 'ch', 'sh', 'ss', 's' or 'x' need to add the suffix –es.

> **Key Point**
>
> To make a word plural, add –s or –es, e.g. sword/ swords, box/boxes.

The suffix –s or –es is also added to a verb when it is in the third person (he, she or it).

Example

When Arthur <u>pulls</u> the sword out, he <u>watches</u> it.

> **Key Point**
>
> Add an 's' or 'es' to a verb with he/ she/it, e.g. pull<u>s</u>, watch<u>es</u>.

The Prefix un-

A **prefix** is added at the beginning of a word to make a new word, e.g. *un- + kind = unkind*. You do not need to change the spelling of a word when you add a prefix.

The prefix *un-* at the beginning of a word means 'not'.

Example

Legends are traditional stories but some parts are <u>untrue</u>.

untrue = not true

Quick Test

1. Add –s or –es to these words to make them plural:
   a) bus **b)** stone **c)** bench
2. Where do you add a suffix?
3. What does the prefix 'un-' mean?

> **Key Words**
>
> • Suffix
> • Verb
> • Adjective
> • Noun
> • Plural
> • Prefix

33

Handwriting

- Form lower case letters and capital letters
- Produce joined-up writing
- Form number digits

Printing Letters

You use **letters** when you write. Every letter has a **capital** form and a **lower case** form. All the letters in the example box below are printed.

Example

Here are the capital letters:

A B C D E F G H I J K L M N O P Q R S T U V W X Y Z

Here are the lower case letters:

a b c d e f g h i j k l m n o p q r s t u v w x y z

Some letters have **descenders**. This means part of the letter goes down below the line that you write on.

Example

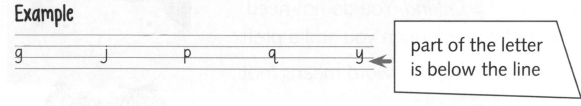

g   j   p   q   y

part of the letter is below the line

Some letters have **ascenders**. This means part of the letter goes up above the line.

Example

b   d   f   h   k   l   t

part of the letter is above the line

All the other letters are written between the lines:

Example

a c e i m n o r s u v w x z

Joined-up Writing

Handwriting can be joined up. But some letters should not be joined to the next letter, such as *v* to *i* and *r* to *a*.

A capital letter should not be joined to lower case letters.

Example

Albert went home.

With some letters (like the letters 'g' and 'f') you loop round to join the other letters.

Example

Imogen ran.

Always leave a space between words.

Numbers

Numbers are used to show an amount or quantity. You need to be able to write numbers correctly.

Example

0 1 2 3 4 5 6 7 8 9

	Star jumps
Alfie	7
Sarah	5
Asif	9
Imogen	3

Tip

You need to sit correctly at a table. Are you holding your pencil comfortably and correctly?

Numbers show an amount of something, such as how many jumps each child did in a PE lesson.

Key Words

- Letter
- Capital letters
- Lower case letters
- Descenders
- Ascenders

Quick Test

1. What letter comes after the letter 'c' in the alphabet?
2. Which seven letters of the alphabet have ascenders?
3. What number comes after 5?

35

Spelling Rules

- Understand rules with vowels
- Recognise how vowels work together

Rules with Vowels

Each **vowel** has a name and a sound.

Example

a apple

e egg

i ink

o orange

u up

These vowel sounds can sometimes be written differently:

Example

ea head thread

y symbol gym

a want watch

o other

- The 'e' sound can be written 'ea'.
- The 'i' sound can be written 'y'.
- The 'o' sound can be written 'a'.
- The 'u' sound can be written 'o'.

The sound of letters can change depending on the letters that come after.

Sometimes two or three letters can show one sound.

Example

All of the following letter combinations make the sound of the name of the letter:

Key Point

A single sound can be made from groups of two or three letters.

a	e	i	o	u
a – e	e – e	i – e	o – e	u – e
made	these	five	home	June
ai	ee	ie	oa	oo
rain	see	lie	boat	food
ay	ea	igh	oe	ue
day	sea	night	toe	blue
A	ie	y	ow	ew
April	chief	cry	own	new
	ey			ou
	key			you

Key Point

The magic 'e' makes the vowel that comes before the magic 'e' say its name not its sound.

Tricky Sounds

Some words use different combinations of letters to make the same sound.

Example

ear	are	air	
bear	bare	fair	
or	ore	ar	aw
for	more	war	saw
er	ir	ur	or
term	girl	Thursday	word
ou	ow		
about	now		
oi	oy		
oil	boy		

Quick Test

1. What are the five different letter combinations that make the sound of the name of the letter 'e'?

Key Word

• Vowel

More Spelling Rules

- Understand rules with consonants
- Spell the days of the week

Rules with Consonants

A **consonant** is any letter that is not a vowel (a, e, i, o, u).

Different consonants can make the same sound.

Sometimes a single sound is produced from two consonants together, such as 'ph', 'gh' or 'th'.

Sometimes a single sound is produced from three consonants together, such as 'tch'.

Key Point

Apart from a, e, i, o and u, all the letters in the alphabet are consonants.

c (as in cat)	f (as in fat)	j (as in jacket)	l (as in lamp)	n (as in nose)
k kitchen	ph alphabet	g giant	le table	kn knock
		-ge age	el camel	gn gnaw
		-dge badge	al metal	
			il April	

r (as in right)	s (as in sea)	sh (as in shoe)	tch (as in fetch	
wr write	c city	-tio station	-ch riches	
	c fancy	-sio television		
		-s sure		

Key Point

Sometimes two or three letters can represent one sound.

Spelling the Days of the Week

You should learn how to spell the days of the week, as they are words you will probably use a lot.

Here are some tips to help you remember how to spell the days of the week:
- They all end in the word **day**.
- They all start with a capital letter.
- Five days have two syllable 'beats'. (Monday, Tuesday, Thursday, Friday, Sunday)

Tip

Which sounds do you know in the word? Segment the word into smaller parts. Say the word aloud.

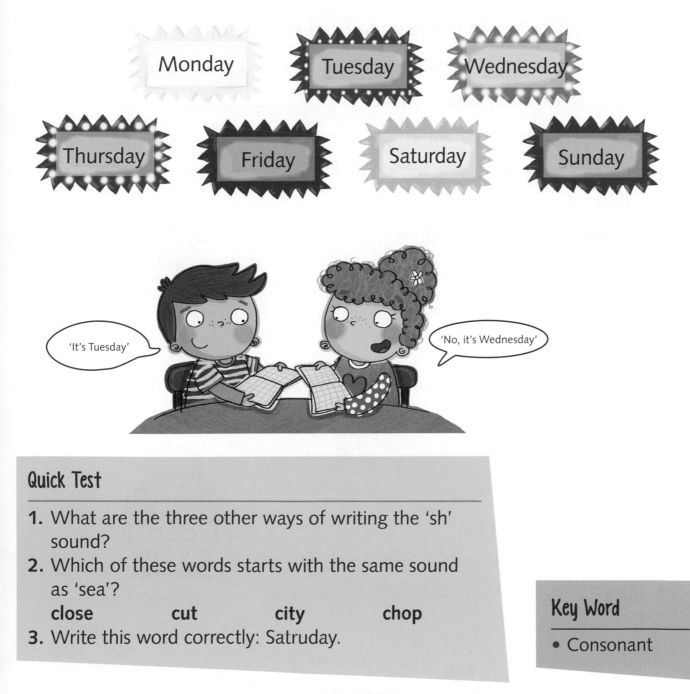

Monday   Tuesday   Wednesday

Thursday   Friday   Saturday   Sunday

'It's Tuesday'   'No, it's Wednesday'

Quick Test

1. What are the three other ways of writing the 'sh' sound?
2. Which of these words starts with the same sound as 'sea'?

   close   **cut**   **city**   **chop**
3. Write this word correctly: Satruday.

Key Word
- Consonant

Practice Questions

Challenge 1

G) Grammar   P) Punctuation   S) Spelling

G **1** Read the sentences and underline the correct word.

a) **One / Won** day, Goldilocks went for a walk.

b) **Their / There** was a house.

c) It belonged to the three **bears / bares**.

d) **Hear / Here** is the house.

4 marks

Challenge 2

GS **1** Choose a suffix to add to the underlined word. Write the correct word.

a) Goldilocks is <u>go</u> for a walk.   _____

b) She is <u>sit</u> on baby bear's chair.   _____

c) The bears are <u>take</u> a walk.   _____

3 marks

S **2** Choose the correct vowels for each word and write them in the space provided.

a) **ou / oo**   w__ __ d

b) **ai / ie**   cr__ __ s

c) **ou / ow**   h__ __ se

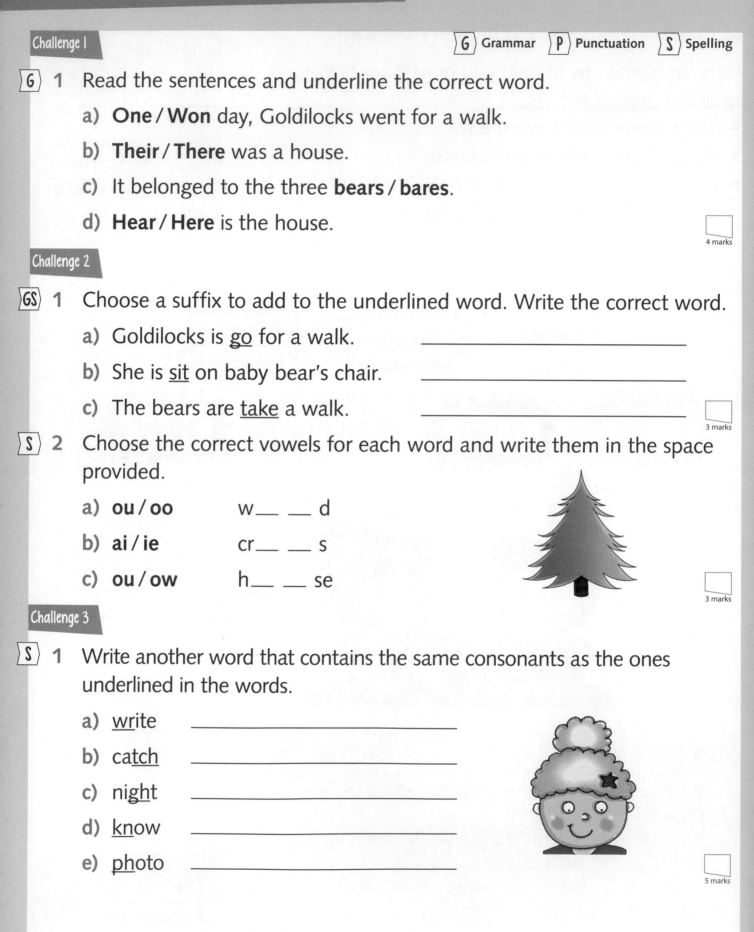

3 marks

Challenge 3

S **1** Write another word that contains the same consonants as the ones underlined in the words.

a) <u>wr</u>ite   _____

b) ca<u>tch</u>   _____

c) nigh<u>t</u>   _____

d) <u>kn</u>ow   _____

e) <u>ph</u>oto   _____

5 marks

Review Questions

1 Read the text. Tick (✓) the sentence that is true.

> People say they have seen a monster in Loch Ness. Maybe a dinosaur still lives there in the deep water of the loch. Submarines have searched for it but we still don't know for sure.

a) A dinosaur lives in Loch Ness. ☐

b) The words 'say' and 'maybe' mean it is a fact. ☐

c) Submarines can work in deep water. ☐

d) We can see other live dinosaurs in the UK. ☐

☐ 1 mark

2 Read the sentences and tick the text type.

	Explanation	Information	Instructions
a) Cheetahs can run up to 120 kilometres per hour.	☐	☐	☐
b) Bees pollinate our plants by flying from flower to flower.	☐	☐	☐
c) Chop the onions.	☐	☐	☐

☐ 3 marks

3 Read the poem.

a) Circle any rhyming words.

b) Underline any repetitive words.

> Little drops of water,
>
> Little grains of sand,
>
> Make the mighty ocean
>
> And the pleasant land.

☐ 5 marks

Planning and Checking Your Writing

- Collect and draft ideas
- Re-read your writing to check meaning is clear

Getting Ideas

Whenever you start writing, it is always good to have a 'starting point' or an exciting idea.

It is important to ask yourself lots of questions to get ideas.

Example

Ben is having a party for his birthday.
- **Who** will go to the party?
- **What** will people wear?
- **What** presents will people take?
- **How** will people get to the party?

Ideas do not need to be organised or written in detail. Use bullet points or a **thought shower** to help you to jot down your ideas.

Example

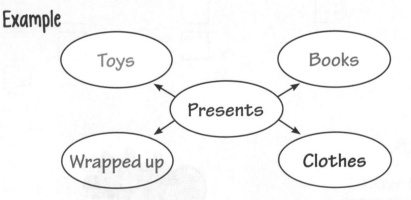

Drafting Your Writing

Drafting is the first time that you put your ideas into sentences.

You must think about the purpose of your writing. What are you writing for? For example, are you writing to explain something or to entertain people?

Key Point

Ideas should be quick and short, so don't waste time writing full sentences. Just write key words.

Tip

Try to use varied and interesting words. For example, instead of 'big', use 'enormous' or 'huge'.

Re-reading

When you have finished writing, read your writing again. Check that it makes sense and that you have included all your ideas. This is called **proofreading**. You can **edit** any mistakes.

A proofreading check list should include:

- Have you used capital letters and full stops?
- Have you used interesting words?
- Have you written with a purpose?
- Does your writing make sense?

Example

You might write a letter to tell somebody something.

> Dear Ben,
>
> i am writing to tell you that i would love to come to your party it was very kind of you to invite me to join you

> What time does the party begin

> Thank you again. I am really looking forward to it.
> Kaind regards,
> Billy Night

Tip

Re-read your writing out loud. Check that it makes sense.

Check for missing capital letters and full stops.

Check for missing question marks.

Check spelling.

Quick Test

1. What techniques could you use to jot down your ideas?
2. What is drafting?
3. What is proofreading?

Key Words

- Thought shower
- Drafting
- Proofreading
- Editing

Writing Fiction and Non-fiction

- Know how to write a story
- Know how to write about real people
- Use paragraphs
- Join sentences

Writing Fiction

A made-up story is called **fiction**. A story can be about anyone or anything that you make up.

A 'story mountain' can help you to organise your ideas.

Example

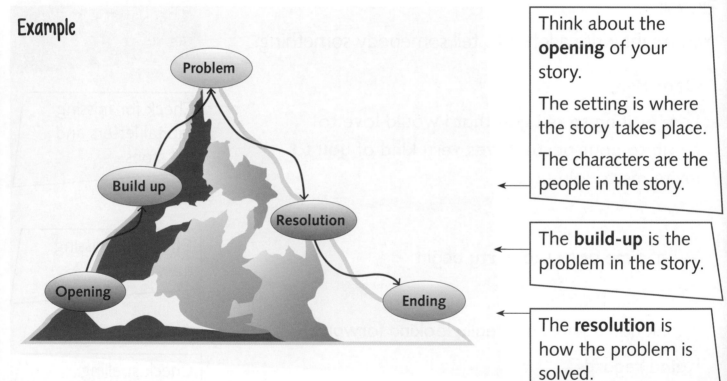

Think about the **opening** of your story.

The setting is where the story takes place.

The characters are the people in the story.

The **build-up** is the problem in the story.

The **resolution** is how the problem is solved.

Writing Non-fiction

Non-fiction is about real things or real people. An autobiography is a piece of writing about yourself. A biography is a piece of writing about someone else.

When you write about someone else, you may need to find facts from secondary sources. Secondary sources are books, videos or the Internet. Primary sources are first-hand experiences or information, such as a diary.

Key Point

Fiction is a 'made-up' story. Non-fiction is about real people or a real event.

You could draw a thought shower (mind map) to collect ideas.

Example

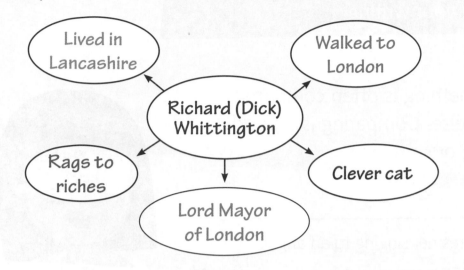

Tip

It is useful to make notes from secondary sources. But do not print or copy pages of information. Pick out the useful facts that interest you.

Using Paragraphs and Joining Sentences

You should write in **paragraphs**. Start a new paragraph when you write about a different event, person or place.

You can link your sentences by using words such as 'first', 'then' and 'finally'. These words organise your sentences in time order.

Example

> **First**, he put his possessions in a knapsack. **Then,** he and his cat walked to London.
>
> **Finally**, he became Lord Mayor of London.

Key Point

Divide your writing into paragraphs. You begin a new paragraph on a new line.

Quick Test

1. Give an example of a word used to link sentences.
2. Give an example of non-fiction writing.

Key Words

- Fiction
- Non-fiction
- Paragraph

Poetry Features

- Use comparison and imagery in your writing
- Use rhyming patterns in your writing

Comparing

In poetry, someone or something is often compared to someone or something else. Comparing is a good way to describe something or someone.

Example

She sang like an angel.

Compares her singing to an angel.

Comparisons are important in poetry as they help the reader to see and feel the words.

Example

The moon was a silver ball,
Glowing very bright,
And not small at all,
In the middle of the night.

The moon is being compared to a ball in this poem.

You can compare characters to other people or to objects.

Example

That child was a walking dictionary.

A clever child is being compared to a dictionary full of information.

Imagery

Imagery is when words create a picture in the reader's mind. Imagery is used to describe a person, place or thing using sight, smell, taste, sound and touch.

Example

The sharp edge of the party invitation cut my finger and made it sting.

One bite of the sour lemon made my lips pucker.

I love the sweet smell of freshly baked cookies.

> **Touch** imagery.

> **Taste** imagery.

> **Smell** imagery.

Using Rhyming Patterns

Rhyming words have endings that sound the same. They often come at the end of lines of poetry and they follow a **rhyming pattern**.

Tip

Which words make a picture in your mind? Which sense do you feel it through?

Example

The boy found a **sweet**	A
Lying on the **street**.	A
He made a **wish**	B
And shouted,	
'Mmmm, **delish**!'	B

> A rhyming **couplet** is when two lines in a poem, one after the other, have the same sound at the end (AABB).

Other rhyming patterns are ABAB and ABCB.

Example

The birthday girl was called **Mandy**.	A
The party was in the **park**.	B
She was treated with lots of **candy**,	A
From dawn until **dark**.	B

> This poem has an ABAB rhyming pattern. If the word 'candy' was replaced with 'sweets', the poem would have an ABCB rhyming pattern (where only the second and last lines rhyme).

Quick Test

1. What is imagery?
2. Name two rhyming patterns.

Key Words

- Imagery
- Rhyming pattern
- Couplets

Writing for Different Purposes

- Write a book review
- Write a character profile
- Write a recount

Book Reviews

You write a **book review** to share your opinion of a book after you have read it.

You need to include these things in your review and give reasons where you can:
- What is the title of the book?
- Who is the author?
- Who is the illustrator?
- What is your favourite part in the book? Why?
- Who are the main characters?
- Did you like the illustrations?
- Did you enjoy the book? Why?
- Who else might like this book?
- You might also want to give it a star rating (e.g. out of 5).

Key Point

In a book review you must try to give reasons for your statements.

Character Profiles

A character profile is a description of a character in a story. Try to think of powerful **adjectives** to describe the character, so that readers want to read the story too.

Example

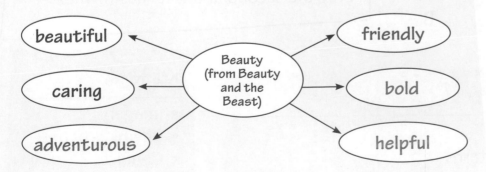

- beautiful
- friendly
- caring
- bold
- adventurous
- helpful

Beauty (from Beauty and the Beast)

Key Point

Always use interesting adjectives to describe characters.

Recounts

A **recount** is written using 'I' or 'we'. It is a way of re-telling an important event or experience you have had.

You use the **past tense** because the event has already happened. You make the past tense by adding 'ed' to the end of most verbs.

Example

- walk + ed ⟶ walked
- jump + ed ⟶ jumped

But remember that some verbs don't follow this pattern, e.g.

- see ⟶ saw
- go ⟶ went

You can use **time connectives** to put the events in your recount in order:

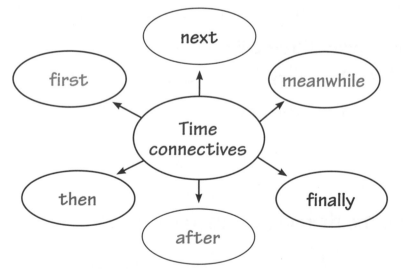

Key Point

You can make many verbs past tense by adding 'ed'.

Quick Test

1. What is a book review?
2. What type of words should you use when you describe characters?
3. What tense do you use in a recount?

Key Words

- Book review
- Adjective
- Recount
- Past tense
- Time connectives

49

Practice Questions

Challenge 1

1 Look at the thought shower (mind map) about Florence Nightingale.
   Write the question words next to the text.

where   what   when

a) 1820–1910   b) Training nurses

_____   _____

c) Crimean War   Florence
                             Nightingale

_____

3 marks

Challenge 2

1 Read the texts a)–c), then match them with the headings.

opening   build-up   resolution

a) One day, they decided to cross the bridge.
    "Who's on MY bridge?" growled the Troll. _____

b) Once upon a time, there were three Billy
    Goats who lived in a field in a valley.   _____

c) Finally, the Billy Goats sent the Troll into
    the deep valley below.   _____

3 marks

Challenge 3

1 Read the poems. Underline the rhyming words in each poem.

a)   b)

6 marks

Little Star,   Up there,
Don't go far.   High up on a hill,
Can you see me?   I saw an owl,
Through the tree.   Next to a mill.

G Grammar   P Punctuation   S Spelling

GS 1 Choose the suffix **–ment** or **–ness** for the underlined word. Write the word.

a) Arthur got a lot of <u>enjoy</u> from owning the sword.

_____

b) 'Gosh, he's done it!' said the people with <u>excite</u>.

_____

c) 'Let's steal it,' said one knight with <u>wicked</u>.

_____

d) Suddenly Arthur saw a <u>move</u> to his right.

_____   **4 marks**

GS 2 Choose the suffix **–s** or **–es** for the underlined word. Write the word.

a) Arthur <u>take</u> the sword from the stone.   _____

b) He <u>wish</u> he hadn't!   _____

c) The sword <u>feel</u> heavy in his hands.   _____

d) Arthur <u>search</u> for a safe place to put it.   _____

e) Merlin <u>fuss</u> about keeping it safe.   _____   **5 marks**

3 Write the missing letters of the alphabet.

a____ c____ e f____ h i____ k l m n o ____ ____ r s t u v w x y z   **6 marks**

4 Read the words, then write the numbers.

a) two   _____

b) five   _____

c) three   _____   **3 marks**

5 Read the numbers, then write the missing numbers.

1 2 3 4 5 ____ 7 8 ____ 10   **2 marks**

Capital Letters and Punctuation

- Use capital letters and full stops in simple sentences
- Use question marks and exclamation marks
- Use commas to separate items in a list

Using Capital Letters and Full Stops

The word at the beginning of a sentence always starts with a **capital letter.**

Example

- **A**ll sentences start with a capital letter. ✓
- **a**ll sentences start with a capital letter. ✗

Capital letters are used for names of people and places, for days of the week and months of the year.

Example

- Lions are from **A**frica.
- That parrot is an **A**frican **G**rey.
- Today is **W**ednesday.
- My birthday is in **J**anuary.

A capital letter is used for the word 'I'.

Example

- **I** am 7 years old.
- Tom and **I** played football.

A **full stop** (.) is used to end most sentences.

Example

- Sentences end with a full stop. ✓
- Sentences end with a full stop ✗

Using Question Marks and Exclamation Marks

A **question mark** (**?**) is used when asking a question. Questions often start with a question word (who, what, where, why, when and how) and they must end with a question mark.

Example

- **What** does a snake eat**?**
- **How** long do tortoises live**?**

An **exclamation mark** (**!**) is used to show that someone is shouting or is surprised.

Example

- Argh, a snake**!**
- Tortoises can live for 80 years**!**

Using Commas in a List

A **comma** (**,**) separates words in a list. You only use a comma when there are three or more words in the list. You use the word 'and' before the last word in the list.

Example

- A horse eats grass, hay **and** grains.
- Birds eat dried fruit, nuts, seeds **and** worms.

Key Point

Sentences that begin with a question word must end with a question mark. The question words are: **who, what, where, why, when** and **how**.

Tip

Remember to use 'and' before the last word, not a comma, e.g. Snakes eat insects, rodents **and** eggs.

Quick Test

1. When do you use a capital letter?
2. What are the six question words?
3. How many words do you need in a list before you use a comma?

Key Words

- Capital letter
- Full stop
- Question mark
- Exclamation mark
- Comma

Using Tenses and Joining Words

- Use the present and the past tenses
- Use joining words *and*, *or*, *but*
- Use joining words *when*, *if*, *that*, *because*

Present and Past Tenses

The **present tense** is used to talk about the present (now). The **past tense** is used to talk about the past.

You use the present tense to talk about a fact or an action that is true now.

Example

The tortoise and the hare **run** a race.

You use the **present progressive tense** to talk about an action that is happening now – it is still ongoing.

Example

The tortoise and the hare **are running** a race.

You use the past tense to talk about something that has happened.

Example

The hare **ran** past the tortoise.

> **Key Point**
>
> The present and past progressive tenses use two **verbs** together. The second verb always ends in '*ing*'.

You use the **past progressive tense** to talk about an action that was happening in the past.

Example

The hare **was napping** when the tortoise walked past.

Using *and, or, but*

You can often join two sentences together using *and, or* and *but*.

- You use 'and' to join information.
- You use 'or' to show a choice between one thing and another.
- You use 'but' to show different ideas.

Example

- The hare was boastful **and** he lost the race.
- He had to keep going **or** he wouldn't win.
- The tortoise was slow **but** he was steady.

Using *when, if, that, because*

You can often join two **clauses** together using *when, if, that* or *because*.

A clause is a group of words containing a subject (the main person or thing in the sentence) and a verb.

Example

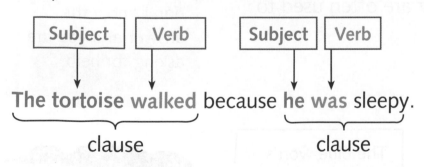

Key Point

A clause has a subject and a verb.

Key Words

- Present tense
- Past tense
- Present progressive tense
- Verb
- Past progressive tense
- Clause

Quick Test

1. Which tense do you use for something that has already happened?
2. Which tense do you use for something that is still happening now?
3. What do the words *and, or, but* do?

Different Types of Sentence

- Write statements
- Write questions and exclamations
- Write commands

Statements

A **statement** is a clear and definite sentence in either writing or speech.

Example

- The pet hamster has small, sharp teeth.
- It answers to the name Harry.
- The children are worried because he is missing.

Questions

A **question** is used when someone is asking for information. A question has a **question mark** (?) at the end.

There are six question words that are often used to form a question.

Key Point

Questions are used to show that you don't know the answer and you are asking for help.

Example

- **Who** is looking for it?
- **What** does it like to eat?
- **Where** might it be hiding?
- **Why** has it run away?
- **When** did it go missing?
- **How** did Harry escape?

The blue words are question words. They are often used to form questions.

Exclamations

An **exclamation** is used when something is being emphasised or stressed.

An exclamation has an **exclamation mark** (**!**) at the end. It shows a strong feeling, such as surprise, anger or joy.

Example

- How wonderful to see you!
- I can hear him squeaking!

Exclamation marks can also be written in speech and tell you how something is being said.

Example

'I found him!' shouted Molly with excitement.

Commands

A **command** is used to make requests, give instructions and give orders.

- A request is when you ask for something, politely.
- An instruction tells you how to do something.
- An order is a strong command.

Example

- Molly, please don't try to touch him.
- Handle him gently.
- Molly, be careful!

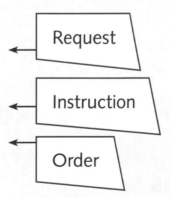

Tip

Think of using an exclamation mark as shouting or raising your voice when speaking.

Key Point

Exclamation marks are used to show emotion.

Key Point

A request is a polite command; it ends with a full stop.

An order is a strong command; it ends with an exclamation mark.

Key Words

- Statement
- Question
- Question mark
- Exclamation
- Exclamation mark
- Command

Quick Test

1. Which of these is a command?
   Go home! / What time is it? / I went to school.
2. When is an exclamation mark used?
3. When is a question mark used?

Types of Words

- Recognise different types of words
- Change verbs into adjectives
- Make comparisons by adding *-er* or *-est* to words
- Change adjectives into adverbs by adding *–ly*

Types of Words

- A **verb** is an action or doing word, e.g. walk, sing.
- A **noun** is a naming word for a person, place or thing, e.g. boy, field, London, pen.
- An **adjective** is a describing word. It tells you more about a noun, e.g. small, red, beautiful. An adjective always comes before the noun.
- An **adverb** describes a verb, e.g. quickly, loudly.

Changing Verbs into Adjectives

You can sometimes change a verb into an adjective by adding the suffix *–ful* or *–less*.

Example

'help' and 'fear' are verbs.
- help + *ful* = helpful (adjective)
- fear + *less* = fearless (adjective)

Jessica was a very **helpful** and **fearless** little girl.

> **Key Point**
>
> You can sometimes turn verbs into adjectives by adding *–ful* and *–less*.

> The adjectives come before the noun.

Making Comparisons

When you want to compare two things, you add the suffix *–er*, for example, 'bigger', 'hotter', 'slower'.

When you want to say something is 'the most', you add *–est*, for example, 'biggest', 'hottest', 'slowest'.

> **Key Point**
>
> You can use adjectives to compare things by adding *–er* and *–est*.

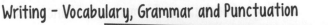

Revise

If the word ends with a 'y' you change the 'y' to an 'i' and then add –*er* or –*est*, e.g. lonely ⟶ loneliest.

Sometimes you need to double the last consonant, e.g. fat ⟶ fattest

Example

Jack was braver than Mila when he went into the darkest cave.

- brav~~e~~ + **er** = braver
- dark + **est** = darkest

> 'brave' ends with an 'e' so you remove the 'e' before adding 'er'.

In the forest lived the scariest wolf.

> 'scary' ends in 'y' so change the 'y' to 'i' before adding 'est'.

The wolf had the biggest ears.

> 'big' ends in a consonant so double it before adding 'est'.

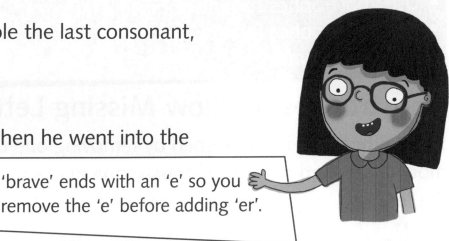

Exceptions to the rule include:
- good ⟶ better ⟶ best
- bad ⟶ worse ⟶ worst
- far ⟶ further ⟶ furthest

Changing Adjectives into Adverbs

You can change some adjectives into adverbs by adding –*ly*.

Example

slow + **ly** = slowly

Jack **slowly** stepped back.

Key Point

You can turn some adjectives into adverbs by adding –*ly*.

Quick Test

What word types are these words?
a) coat   **b)** jumped   **c)** shell   **d)** quickly
e) quick   **f)** better   **g)** coldest

Key Words

- Verb
- Noun
- Adjective
- Adverb

Apostrophes and Noun Phrases

- Use apostrophes to replace missing letters
- Use apostrophes to show belonging
- Use noun phrases in a sentence

Apostrophes to Show Missing Letters

Some words can be shortened by removing one or more letters and adding an **apostrophe** in place of the letter(s).

Example

I've = I have

she's = she has

she'll = she will

they'll = they will

I'm = I am

we're = we are

don't = do not

didn't = did not

mustn't = must not

could've = could have

Key Point

Apostrophes are used to replace letters and to show that something belongs to someone or something.

Apostrophes to Show Belonging

The apostrophe is used to show that something belongs to someone or something.

Example

Pandora + **'s** = Pandora's box ← The box belongs to Pandora.

box + **'s** = box's secret ← The secret belongs to the box.

Tip

Don't confuse **'s** with making a word **plural**.

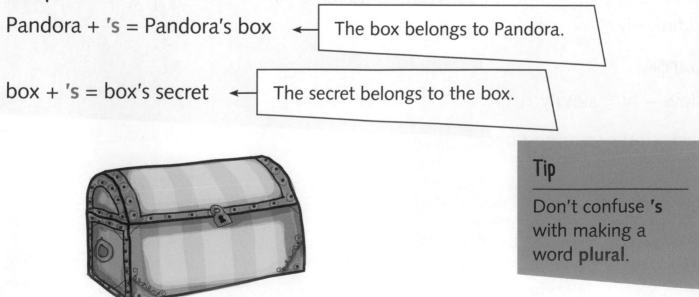

Noun Phrases

A **noun phrase** has a **noun** (a person, place or thing) or pronoun (e.g. he, she, it) and the words that describe the noun or pronoun.

A pronoun is a word that can replace a noun, for example 'he', 'she', 'it', 'they'.

The words 'a' and 'the' are often part of a noun phrase.

The words that describe the noun or pronoun are called **adjectives** and are also part of the noun phrase. They tell you more about the noun.

Example

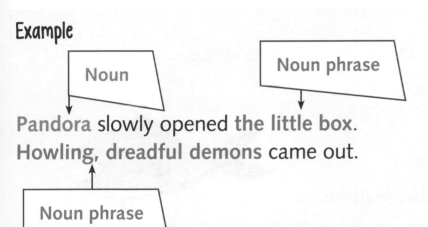

Noun

Noun phrase

Pandora slowly opened **the little box**.
Howling, dreadful demons came out.

Noun phrase

In this example, the words 'little', 'Howling' and 'dreadful' are adjectives and are part of the noun phrases. The words 'box' and 'demons' are nouns.

> **Key Point**
>
> A noun is a naming word. A pronoun is a word that can replace a noun, e.g. he, she, it, they.

Quick Test

1. Write 'could not' as a contraction.
2. Put the apostrophe of belonging into the sentence:

   The box was Pandoras.

3. What is the adjective in this noun phrase?

   the young girl

Key Words

- Apostrophe
- Plural
- Noun phrase
- Noun
- Adjective

Practice Questions

G Grammar   P Punctuation   S Spelling

P **1** Read the sentences. Copy them, adding capital letters and full stops.

a) the bengal tiger is found in india

_____

_____

4 marks

b) i've seen the tigers at london zoo

_____

_____

4 marks

Challenge 2

P **1** Add a punctuation mark at the end of each sentence.

a) What kind of animal is a Golden Eagle

b) That's enormous

2 marks

G **2** Circle the correct word in bold.

a) Birds lay eggs **and/or** have feathers.

b) Fish don't have feathers **but/or** they do lay eggs.

2 marks

Challenge 3

GPS **1** Write two sentences to describe your favourite animal using:
- one word containing an apostrophe to show missing letters
- one adjective
- one adverb.

_____

_____

_____

_____

_____

3 marks

Review Questions

G) Grammar   P) Punctuation   S) Spelling

1 Read the sentences. Put them in the right order by numbering them 1–6. The first one has been done for you.

a) Dick Whittington decided to go to London to find his fortune.   `1`

b) After that, they started the walk to London.

c) Then, he put his things into a knapsack.

d) Finally, they reached London.

e) First, he called his cat.

f) On the way, they slept under a hedge.   `5 marks`

2 Read the questions and circle the correct answers.

a) What kind of narrative is a fairy story?

  Fiction   Non-fiction

b) What is a group of sentences about one idea?

  Paragraph   Noun

c) Which of these words means 'to work out what might happen next in a story'?

  Dictate   Predict   `3 marks`

G) **3** Read the sentences. Tick (✓) the sentences that are true and cross (✗) the ones that are false.

a) A recount is written in the first person using 'I' or 'we'.

b) You usually add –ed to make the past tense.

c) A character profile is a description of a place.   `3 marks`

Review Questions

G Grammar   P Punctuation   S Spelling

G **1** Read the sentence. Draw lines to match each word with its word type.

The clever cat quickly catches the mouse.

| cat | clever | quickly | catches |

| adverb | adjective | verb | noun |

4 marks

SP **2** Copy the sentences, adding punctuation marks.

a) the smallest snake is the size of a toothpick

_____

_____

2 marks

b) do you know snakes live in rivers lakes and swamps

_____

_____

3 marks

P **3** Read the sentences. Tick (✓) the sentence that needs an apostrophe to show belonging. Add the apostrophe.

A snakes fangs are poisonous. ☐

Fangs are sharp and hollow. ☐

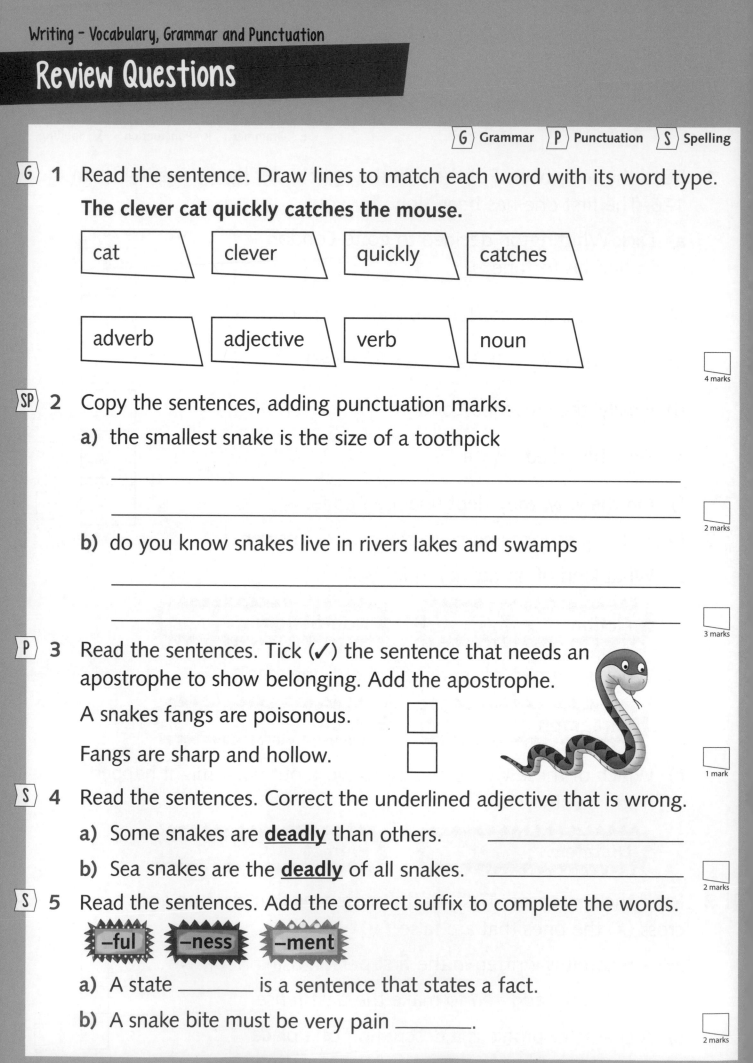

1 mark

S **4** Read the sentences. Correct the underlined adjective that is wrong.

a) Some snakes are **deadly** than others.   _____

b) Sea snakes are the **deadly** of all snakes.   _____

2 marks

S **5** Read the sentences. Add the correct suffix to complete the words.

–ful   –ness   –ment

a) A state _____ is a sentence that states a fact.

b) A snake bite must be very pain _____.

2 marks

Mixed Questions

G) Grammar   P) Punctuation   S) Spelling

1 Read the words. They all end in the suffix *–ed*, but have a different sound.

Draw lines to match the words to the sounds they make at the end.

a) walked   **i)**   *'id'*

b) listened   **ii)** *'t'*

c) spotted   **iii)** *'d'*

3 marks

2 Write the sound that these exception words make at the end.

was   is   his   has   _____

1 mark

3 How many syllables do these words have?

a) pocket   _____

b) happily   _____

2 marks

4 Read the poem. Underline the rhyming words.

> One, two,
> Buckle my shoe
> Three, four,
> Knock on the door

2 marks

5 Read the sentence. Tick (✓) the word that completes the sentence.

The sentence, 'Rain pattered softly on my umbrella.' is an example
of _____ imagery.

touch   ☐

taste   ☐

sound   ☐

1 mark

S) 6 The same two vowels are missing from these three words.
Write in the missing letters.

a) c __ __ l d   **b)** w __ __ l d   **c)** s h __ __ l d

1 mark

Mixed Questions

7 Read the sentences below. Number the recipe instructions to show the order 1, 2, 3, 4.

    a) Finally, bake for 15 minutes.

    b) First, heat the oven to 350 degrees.

    c) Then, add the eggs, water and oil, and beat the mixture.

    d) Next, put the dry ingredients in a bowl.

4 marks

8 Tick (✓) one word to complete the sentence below.

Instructions use simple _____, numbers and pictures.

    a) exclamations

    b) questions

    c) commands

1 mark

9 Draw lines to match the descriptive words to the nouns.

slithery, smooth	grasshopper
glowing, green	cat
cute, curious	snake

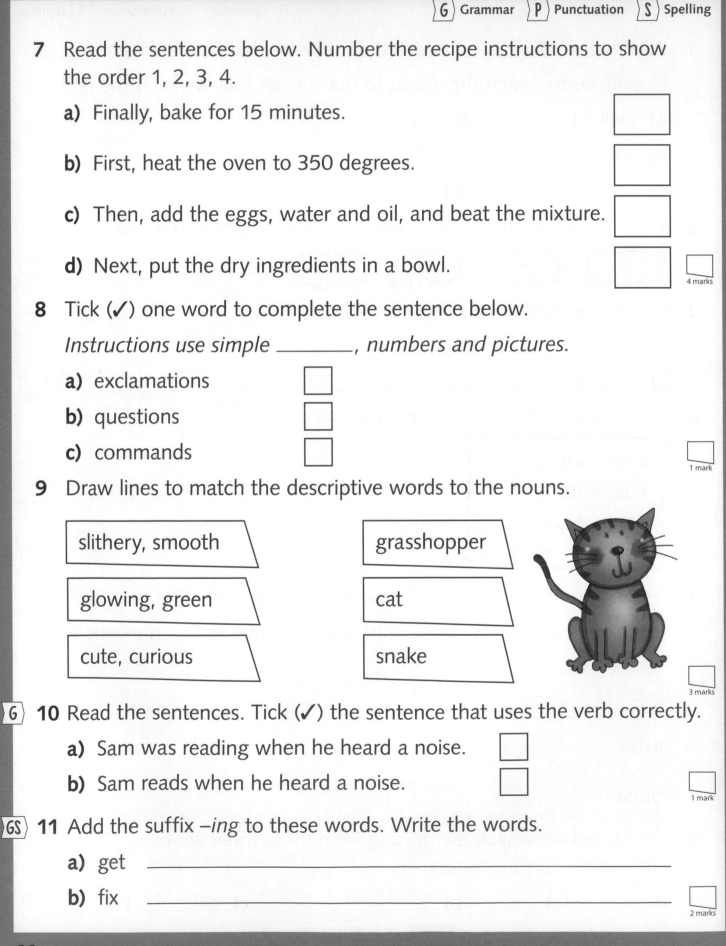

3 marks

G **10** Read the sentences. Tick (✓) the sentence that uses the verb correctly.

    a) Sam was reading when he heard a noise.

    b) Sam reads when he heard a noise.

1 mark

GS **11** Add the suffix *–ing* to these words. Write the words.

    a) get _____

    b) fix _____

2 marks

Mixed Questions

G Grammar P Punctuation S Spelling

12 Read the words and look at the underlined sound.
Circle the word in each set that has a different sound
to the other two.

a) gentle   giraffe   give

b) kitten   circle   cat

c) bread   fed   dream

3 marks

GPS **13** Rewrite the sentences below. Where you can, use words
that contain an apostrophe to show missing letters.

a) I have not brought my umbrella!

_____

_____

b) You are going to get wet!

_____

_____

2 marks

14 Write the missing letters in the alphabetical sequences.

a) g ☐ i ☐ k   b) N ☐ P ☐

4 marks

S **15** Write a word that begins with each of these sounds:

a) *kn* _____

b) *wh* _____

2 marks

S **16** Write a homophone for the word *hear*.

_____

1 mark

S **17** Add the suffix –s or –es to make these words plural. Write the words.

a) toy _____

b) wish _____

2 marks

Mixed Questions

G) Grammar P) Punctuation S) Spelling

S) **18** Add the suffix *–ing* to these words. Write the words.

a) hit _____

b) write _____

2 marks

S) **19** Write a word that ends in the letters '*dge*'.

_____

1 mark

S) **20** Write a word that contains the letters '*ow*'.

_____

1 mark

S) **21** Underline the correct spelling of the word.

a) fatter / fater

b) largest / larggest

c) scaryest / scariest

3 marks

22 Write the numbers. In what year were you born? _____

1 mark

23 Read the texts. Circle the type of book it comes from.

a) Once upon a time, there was a poor boy. **Fiction / Non-fiction**

b) Out of the pupae comes a butterfly. **Fiction / Non-fiction**

c) Salmon swim upstream to lay eggs. **Fiction / Non-fiction**

d) And they lived happily ever after. **Fiction / Non-fiction**

4 marks

P) **24** Add an exclamation mark or a question mark to these sentences.

a) I told you to stop doing that ____

b) Please sir, can I have some more ____

c) Wow ____

d) When will you be home ____

e) What's that terrible smell ____

5 marks

G) Grammar   P) Punctuation   S) Spelling

GS **25** Write the verb shown in brackets in the past tense.

a) The tortoise and the hare (have) _____ a race.

b) The hare (is) _____ very boastful.

c) The hare (think) _____ he would win.

d) The tortoise (walk) _____ slowly past the hare.

4 marks

26 Read the sentences. Add one of the following words in the gaps.

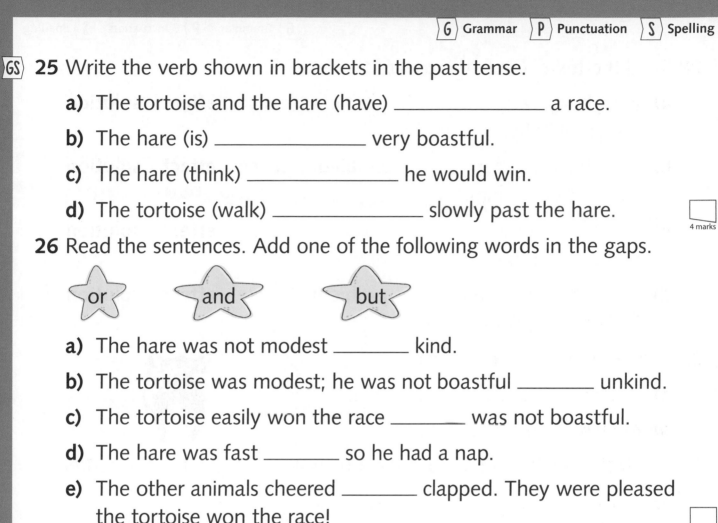

or   and   but

a) The hare was not modest _____ kind.

b) The tortoise was modest; he was not boastful _____ unkind.

c) The tortoise easily won the race _____ was not boastful.

d) The hare was fast _____ so he had a nap.

e) The other animals cheered _____ clapped. They were pleased the tortoise won the race!

5 marks

27 Read the texts. Tick the text type.

	Instructions	Explanation	Information
a) Whisk the egg whites.			
b) Rabbits live in burrows.			
c) A cheetah has spots so it cannot be seen.			

3 marks

Mixed Questions

G) Grammar P) Punctuation S) Spelling

28 Read the texts. Circle the part of the text.

a) Everybody was scared of Toby. problem cause **effect** **solution**

b) Toby barked when you went near him. problem cause **effect** **solution**

c) Ali had a yappy dog called Toby. problem cause **effect** **solution**

d) A dog trainer taught Toby to sit quietly. problem cause **effect** **solution**

4 marks

S) **29** Write the plural of each word.

a) child _____

b) mouse _____

2 marks

S) **30** Read the words. Add 'e' to make a new word. Write it in the sentence.

a) hat + e = _____

I _____ smelly fish!

b) man + e = _____

The horse had a beautiful _____.

2 marks

31 Read the words. Draw lines to show where to segment the sounds.

a) s h o u t   b) p a n   c) t i g h t

3 marks

Page 5 Quick Test
1 3
2 gem
3 **a)** fate **b)** kite

Page 7 Quick Test
1 A syllable is the 'beat' in a word.
2 Examples: **a)** bag
   b) car'pet **c)** yesterday
3 Ho/li/day – 3 syllables

Page 9 Quick Test
1 i
2 **a)** I'll
   b) isn't
   c) it's
3 The fairy's wish was good.

Page 11 Quick Test
1 caring
2 nicer, nicest
3 **a)** fox**es** **b)** bridge**s**

Page 13 Quick Test
1 Plural means more than one.
2 Singular means one.
3 people

Page 14 Quick Test
1 **a)** bed + room **b)** air + port
   c) hill + side
2 Examples: **a)** seaside, seashell
   b) fireplace, firework, fireside
   c) playground, playmate, playtime

Page 15 Practice Questions
Challenge 1
1 **a)** **I'm** so happy.
   b) **We're** happy too.
2 **a)** The Princess was the **Queen's** baby.
   b) It was the bad **fairy's** spindle.

Challenge 2
1 **a)** looked
   b) cared
   c) changing

Challenge 3
1 **a)** 3 syllables: De/cem/ber
   b) 2 syllables: roof/top

2 Examples: **a)** sunshine, sunflower
   b) snowman, snowball
   c) keyhole, keyboard

Page 17 Quick Test
1 At the ends of the lines.
2 A kind of puzzle.
3 me, tree, key

Page 19 Quick Test
1 A problem, a cause, an effect and a solution.
2 Examples: Fairies, Princesses, Witches, Mermaids, Giants.
3 Don't use things that don't belong to you.

Page 21 Quick Test
1 Commands
2 Information text
3 Explanation texts

Page 23 Quick Test
1 Once upon a time;
   They lived happily ever after.
2 Adjectives

Page 25 Quick Test
1 'd' comes first.
2 To find the meanings of words.
3 To find specific information.

Page 27 Quick Test
1 Predict means work out what might happen.
2 facts, pictures

Page 28 Practice Questions
Challenge 1
1 antelope, caterpillar, octopus, tiger, whale

Challenge 2
1 a, d
2 blue – true; road – showed; find – blind

Answers

Challenge 3
1 **a)** starving   **b)** annoyed

Page 29 Review Questions
1 **a)** butter + fly   **b)** black + berry
   c) play + ground   **d)** white + board
   e) foot + ball
2 phone – finger; gentle – jam; city – snake; sugar – shoe; chemist – kitchen
3 **a)** cats   **b)** mice   **c)** men
   d) babies   **e)** elves
4 **a)** 't' sound   **b)** 'd' sound   **c)** 't' sound
   d) 'd' sound **e)** 'id' sound

Page 31 Quick Test
1 Dividing a word into individual sounds and/or syllables.
2 Words that sound the same but have different spellings and meanings.
3 Three sounds (c-u-p)
4 Three sounds (sh-o-p)

Page 33 Quick Test
1 **a)** buses **b)** stones **c)** benches
2 To the end of a word.
3 not

Page 35 Quick Test
1 letter d
2 b, d, f, h, k, l, t
3 number 6

Page 37 Quick Test
1 e – e, ee, ea, ie, ey

Page 39 Quick Test
1 tio, sio, s
2 city
3 Saturday

Page 40 Practice Questions
Challenge 1
1 **a)** One **b)** There **c)** bears **d)** Here

Challenge 2
1 **a)** going **b)** sitting **c)** taking
2 **a)** oo   **b)** ie   **c)** ou

Challenge 3
1 **a)** Examples: wrong, written, wrote, wrap
   b) Examples: match, kitchen, fetch, watch
   c) Examples: knight, light, bright, sight
   d) Examples: knock, knew, knee.
   e) Examples: alphabet; phase; graph; phone.

Page 41 Review Questions
1 **c)** ✓
2 **a)** Information   **b)** Explanation
   c) Instructions
3 **a)** Rhyming words: sand/land;
   b) Repetitive words: little; of; the

Page 43 Quick Test
1 Bullet points or a thought shower/mind map.
2 Drafting is when you put your ideas into sentences.
3 Proofreading means you re-read your writing and edit any mistakes.

Page 45 Quick Test
1 Later, Then, Finally, First, After.
2 Biography, autobiography.

Page 47 Quick Test
1 The use of words to create pictures in the reader's mind.
2 Rhyming couplets (AABB); Rhyme on every other line (ABAB); ABCB.

Page 49 Quick Test
1 A piece of writing about a book you have read. It describes what you liked/didn't like about the book.
2 Adjectives.
3 The past tense.

Page 50 Practice Questions
Challenge 1
1 **a)** when
   b) what
   c) where

Challenge 2
1 a) Build-up   b) Opening
  c) Resolution

Challenge 3
1 a) star/far, me/tree
  b) hill, mill

Page 51 Review Questions
1 a) enjoyment   b) excitement
  c) wickedness   d) movement
2 a) takes   b) wishes
  c) feels   d) searches
  e) fusses
3 a <u>b</u> c <u>d</u> e f g h i <u>j</u> k l m n o p <u>q</u> r s t u v
  w x y z
4 a) 2   b) 5   c) 3
5 1 2 3 4 5 <u>6</u> 7 8 <u>9</u> 10

Page 53 Quick Test
1 To start a sentence, for names of
  people and places, for days of the week,
  months of the year and for the word 'I'.
2 Who, what, where, when, how and why.
3 You only use a comma when there are
  three or more words in a list.

Page 55 Quick Test
1 Past tense
2 Present progressive tense
3 They join two sentences together.

Page 57 Quick Test
1 Go home!
2 An exclamation/strong command/order.
3 At the end of a question.

Page 59 Quick Test
1 a) noun   b) verb   c) noun
  d) adverb   e) adjective f) adjective
  g) adjective

Page 61 Quick Test
1 couldn't
2 The box was Pandora's.
3 young

Page 62 Practice Questions
Challenge 1
1 a) The Bengal tiger is found in India.
  b) I've seen the tigers at London Zoo.

Challenge 2
1 a) ?   b) !
2 a) and   b) but

Challenge 3
1 1 mark each for correct use of word
  containing an apostrophe to show
  missing letters, one adjective and one
  adverb. Example: Cats are my favourite
  animal because they're cute. They purr
  loudly and have soft fur.

Page 63 Review Questions
1 a) 1   b) 4   c) 3
  d) 6   e) 2   f) 5
2 a) Fiction b) Paragraph c) Predict
3 a) ✓   b) ✓   c) ✗

Page 64 Review Questions
1 cat – noun; clever – adjective;
  quickly – adverb; catches – verb
2 a) The smallest snake is the size of a
     toothpick!
  b) Do you know snakes live in rivers,
     lakes and swamps?
3 A snake's fangs are poisonous. ✓
4 a) deadlier   b) deadliest
5 a) statement b) painful

Page 65–70 Mixed Questions
1 a) walked –   ii) 't'
  b) listened – iii) 'd'
  c) spotted –   i) 'id'
2 'z'
3 a) 2
  b) 3
4 two, shoe; four, door
5 sound
6 ou
7 a) 4   b) 1
  c) 3   d) 2

Answers

8 **c)** commands

9 slithery, smooth – snake
glowing, green – grasshopper
cute, curious – cat

10 **a)** ✓

11 **a)** getting **b)** fixing

12 **a)** give **b)** circle **c)** dream

13 **a)** I haven't brought my umbrella!
b) You're going to get wet!

14 **a)** h j **b)** O Q

15 **a)** Examples: know, knew, knight, knot
b) Examples: who, what, why,
where, when

16 here

17 **a)** toys **b)** wishes

18 **a)** hitting **b)** writing

19 Examples: edge, hedge, wedge, ledge

20 towel, sow, bow, grow, throw

21 **a)** fatter **b)** largest
c) scariest

22 Correct year of birth.

23 **a)** Fiction **b)** Non-fiction
c) Non-fiction **d)** Fiction

24 **a)** ! **b)** ? **c)** ! **d)** ? **e)** ?

25 **a)** had **b)** was
c) thought **d)** walked

26 **a)** or **b)** or **c)** but
d) and **e)** and

27 **a)** Instructions **b)** Information
c) Explanation

28 **a)** effect **b)** cause
c) problem **e)** solution

29 **a)** children **b)** mice

30 **a)** hate **b)** mane

31 **a)** sh/ou/t **b)** p/a/n **c)** t/igh/t

A

Adjective	These are sometimes called 'describing words' because they pick out things such as size and colour. They always comes before a noun, or after the verb 'be'.
Adverb	A word used to describe the way you do something, e.g. loudly, slowly, and it can also be used to describe time, e.g. soon, often, later.
Alliteration	Words that start with the same letter or sound, e.g. slimy snails slither slowly.
Alphabetical order	The order of the letters in the alphabet.
Apostrophe	These have two uses: 1) replacing missing letters, e.g. I'm = I am, 2) showing belonging e.g. Hannah's mother.
Ascenders	The part of a lower case letter that rises above the line, e.g. *b, d, f, h*.

B

Book review	A description of a book – what you like and what you don't like and why.

C

Capital letter	A letter of the alphabet that usually differs from the lower case letter in form and height, e.g. A a, B b, Q q.
Clause	A group of words containing a subject and a verb.
Comma	A mark of punctuation (,) used to show a division in a sentence.
Commands	Orders, e.g. Stop that now!
Compound words	Words made from two or more other words, e.g., *class/room, white/board*.
Consonant	The letters of the alphabet which are not vowels.
Contents	A list of all chapters/parts of the book with their page numbers.
Couplet	Two lines of a poem which have rhyming words at the end. (AA BB)

D

Descenders	The part of a lower case letter that goes below the line, e.g. *p, q, j* or *y*.
Dictionary	A book that contains a list of words in alphabetical order and explains their meanings.
Drafting	Creating a first draft of writing.

E

Editing	Revising or correcting your writing.
Exception words	Words in which the English spelling code works in an uncommon way, e.g. *the, do, of, are*.
Exclamation	A phrase or sentence where a thought or feeling is being highlighted or emphasised, e.g. Get out!
Exclamation mark	A punctuation mark (!) used in writing after an exclamation, e.g. *Wow! That was fast!*

Glossary

F

Fairy story	A story, usually for children, about elves, goblins, dragons, fairies or other magical creatures, e.g. *Snow white and the Seven Dwarves*.
Fiction	An imaginative story, a made-up story, e.g. *Cinderella*.
Free verse	Contemporary poems which do not have a rhyme or rhythm.
Full stop	A punctuation mark (.) used at the end of a sentence, e.g. *The fat cat sat on a mat.*

G

Glossary	An alphabetical list of key words and their meanings.

H

Heading	A title for a section of text.
Homophone	Different words that sound exactly the same when pronounced but the spelling is different, e.g. *hear* and *here*.

I

Imagery	Making images, figures or likenesses of things through words.
Index	An alphabetical list of names, places, topics with page numbers.
Information	Knowledge about a particular fact, e.g. *The Earth is round.*
Instructions	Telling someone information or how to do something.

K

Key story	A type of story that can be, e.g., a mystery, adventure or love story.

L

Letter	A symbol of the alphabet that is used in writing and printing to show a speech sound and that is part of an alphabet, e.g. *a, b, c, d,* e.
Lower case letters	Small letters, or symbols, of the alphabet used in writing and printing, e.g. *a, b, c, d,* e.

N

Non-fiction	All writing that is based on facts and reality, including biography and history.
Noun	Sometimes called 'naming words' because they name people, places and things.
Noun phrase	A phrase containing a noun e.g. *Some foxes.*

P

Paragraph	A part of writing with a particular idea, beginning on a new line.
Past progressive tense	Used to talk about an action that was happening in the past.
Past tense	Used to talk about the past.

Plural	More than one. A plural noun normally has a suffix –s or –es. There are a few exceptions, e.g. *mouse – mice*.
Poem	Writing that uses rhythm to express an idea about someone or something.
Predict	To work out or tell in advance, e.g. *I think the rain will stop this afternoon.*
Prefix	A group of letters added to the beginning of a word in order to turn it into another word, e.g. *un- + kind = unkind*.
Present progressive tense	Used to talk about an action that is happening now.
Present tense	Used to talk about the present.
Proofreading	Reading through a piece of writing to find and correct errors.

Q

Question	A sentence used to find more information, often uses question words, e.g. *what*, *where*, *when*, *why*, *where* and *how*.
Question mark	A punctuation mark (?), which shows a question, e.g. *What's this?*

R

Riddle	A statement or a question with a hidden meaning and can be a kind of puzzle, e.g. *What gets wetter as it dries? (a towel)*
Recount	To retell something that has already happened, e.g. *a newspaper report.*
Recurring language	Something (e.g. words, sounds) occurring a number of times in stories or poems.
Rhyme	Words where the ending sounds the same, e.g. *One, two, three, four, five / Once I caught a fish alive.*
Rhyming pattern	A rhyming scheme that shows which letters rhyme in a verse, e.g. ABCB, AABB

A *Baa, baa black sheep*	A *Twinkle, twinkle, little star*
B Have you any wool?	A *How I wonder what you are?*
C Yes sir, yes sir	B *Up above the world so high*
B *Three bags full.*	B *Like a diamond in the sky.*

Rhythm	The beat in a line of a poem.

S

Scan	To read for specific information.
Segment	To separate or divide into smaller chunks, e.g. *seg-men-ting.*
Singular	One person, place, thing or event, e.g. *he, she, it.*
Statement	A clear and definite sentence.
Suffix	A group of letters added to the end of a word to turn it into another word, e.g. +*-ing, -ed, -er* or *–est.*
Syllable	A 'beat' in a word. Syllables contain a vowel sound.

Glossary

T

Thought shower	Another term for mind map. A way of planning ideas that you might want to use.
Time connectives	Used to order events in writing, e.g. *first, then, next, after, meanwhile, finally*.
Tongue twisters	A series of words starting with the same sound and spoken quickly so they twist your tongue.
Traditional tale	An old story that has been told many times. It was written to teach a lesson and to pass on ideas.

V

Verb	'Doing words' e.g. running, sing, cooked.
Vowel	The letters, *a, e, i, o,* and *u*.
Vowel sound	The sounds produced from the letters a, e, i, o and u.

W

Word	A unit of language, consisting of one or more spoken sounds or their written symbols. A word carries meaning. Words are separated by spaces in writing.

Index